simple
card
magic
for everyone

simple card magic for everyone

♠

david devine

Foreword by Michael Bailey
Past President of the Magic Circle

foulsham
LONDON • NEW YORK • TORONTO • SYDNEY

foulsham

The Publishing House, Bennetts Close, Cippenham, Slough, Berkshire SL1 5AP, England

ISBN 0-572-03007-X

A CIP record for this book is available from the British Library

Cover photograph © Corbis Picture Library

Printed and bound in Great Britain by Cox & Wyman Ltd, Reading, Berkshire

Contents

Foreword

MICHAEL BAILEY

Past President of *The Magic Circle*

The art of magic has always been popular and never more so than today. To be able to perform a few neat mysteries for your family and friends makes a wonderful and fulfilling hobby, and may even lead to greater things. The best way to start on this fascinating road is to read the right books. *Simple Card Magic for Everyone* is deliberately aimed at the beginner and it will teach you how to perform some excellent card tricks, and help you to become a good magician.

But knowing how a trick is done is only the beginning. The skill executed in concealing the method is important – and constant practice is the key to this - but the real secret lies in how you present the trick. Knowing the routine so well that you can perform it effortlessly means you can concentrate on the presentation. The use of some good patter not only draws the attention away from the moves at the right moment but also provides the sparkle that every trick needs to bring it to life and make it really enjoyable to watch.

One of the first tricks in this book, The Four Jacks, demonstrates that a good storyline combined with mystery produces entertainment value, and transforms you from someone simply showing off a puzzle into a conjuror your friends will want to watch over and over again.

In this book you are given some excellent tricks to get you accustomed to performing card magic. The secrets may be simple but it's the effect on the audience that's important. Audiences love being baffled, but they don't really want to know how the magic's done, so always remember not to reveal the secrets.

Pick out a few favourites from the magical fare that follows. Practise these well and you will be on the way to becoming a successful – and popular - magician. *Simple Card Magic for Everyone* will give you much pleasure and great satisfaction.

Introduction

Here is a book that will have you performing impressive card tricks in half an hour. There are fifty tricks here, baffling to watch but, with a little practice, simple to perform. Most of them can be done with an ordinary pack of cards for an impromptu performance; others need special cards, basic props or an assistant who is in the know. Whether you want to entertain your friends or work up a complete stage act, this is a great place to start.

But first you need to know the basics.

The secret to successful card magic is practice, practice, practice. You need to be completely comfortable with a pack of cards, so while you are watching TV, travelling on a train or whenever you have an idle moment, pick up a pack and practise shuffling, cutting, forming fans, palming and generally manipulating the cards, so that it becomes second nature. As a general rule, tricks should be performed with new cards, because they are slippery and move smoothly. Not only that, but also if you can open a new pack in front of your audience, they will be reassured that you haven't tampered with them in any way. Having said that, there are a few tricks in this book for which old cards are recommended. It is also an idea to keep an old or even incomplete pack for when you need to create particular effects.

Magic shops sell special cards for conjurors, with particular patterns on the back, of different sizes and shapes and with two faces or two backs. Explore the possibilities and extend your repertoire as you become more proficient with the basic pack.

The other key ingredient is to develop your own style. Don't try to be formal if this doesn't come naturally to you. Similarly, don't try to tell jokes as you go along if this is going to distract you. Experiment with various styles of addressing your audience, decide what works for you and stick with it. There are times when you will need to use your patter to divert attention from what your hands are doing. Similarly, wear clothes that are comfortable but that allow for the possibility of concealing cards and other props about your person.

As well as special technical props, you will occasionally need pieces of equipment that it is reasonable to assume you will be able to borrow from your audience, such as pencils or a coin. However, it is well to have your own to hand just in case. After all, how many people these days wear a bowler hat or carry a silk handkerchief in their top pocket?

If you are working on a stage with a small table, it is a good idea to have a permanent trademark prop on it, not only to enhance your stage persona but also to hide various deceptions; perhaps a traditional magician's top hat, a large bunch of flowers or a bottle of wine and a glass – whatever suits your personality.

BASIC TECHNIQUES

Shuffling the cards

The basic way to shuffle cards is overhand. Hold the pack in your right hand at an angle of about forty-five degrees to your left hand. In this position pass the cards, either singly or in small packets, from your right hand to your left, drawing cards off with your left thumb. The method means you are able to keep a card or several cards completely under control without anyone being suspicious, simply by applying pressure where it is needed.

To keep the top card in position, as you lift the pack with your right hand, retain the top card in your left hand by a slight pressure of your left thumb. Shuffle off all the cards on top of this one. Then lift the whole pack with your right hand and shuffle off all the cards into the left to the last card, which you drop on top. Similarly, to retain a card at the bottom of the pack you need only to keep it in your left hand by pressing on it with your fingers. By combining these techniques it is perfectly possible to carry out what looks like a fair shuffle but in which top and bottom cards remain where they are. Practise this by having the top and bottom cards turned the opposite way to the rest of the pack, so that you can see where they are.

Turning a pack

Spread the pack in a wide fan in your left hand from left to right. Close the fan by placing your right hand on the left side of the fan and closing the pack towards the right. Retain your hold on the cards with the thumb and fingers of each hand at the ends.

Palming a card

Palming a card is the act of taking it from the pack and holding it in the hand while other operations are going on, all without anyone being aware of your actions. It is a highly useful accomplishment and one that is not difficult, after a little practice. The palmed card is simply clipped between the ball of the thumb and the top joints of the fingers.

1. To get the card into position, hold the pack, with the card to be palmed on top, in the left hand and cover with the right lengthways.
2. With the thumb of the left hand push the card about 2 cm (³/₄ in) off the pack, and then with the fingers of the left hand underneath and right round the pack push the card upwards into the palm of your right hand.
3. Bend the hand and the card will remain out of sight as long as you keep your fingers close together, knuckles uppermost.

Palming a card

Try sitting with a card in this position while you are watching TV, and it will soon become so comfortable that you don't betray its presence by holding your hand awkwardly.

In all tricks where a spectator has chosen a card and you have got it on to the top of the pack, the art of palming will be extremely helpful. You will be able to allow the spectator to shuffle the pack themselves and to get a sight of the card at the same time.

After the shuffling, take the cards back with the left hand and place them on the palmed card in your right hand. In your first attempts you will find it easiest to do this by pretending to examine the pack held face upwards and fan-wise in both hands, saying, 'Yes, they seem to be very well shuffled indeed.' The act of closing the fan after this will disguise your action in placing the palmed card at the back of the pack.

Simple tricks to get you started

WEIGHING THE CARD

Amaze your audience with the incredible sensitivity of your fingertips.

1. Allow someone to hand you any card they like from a pack – or, if you want to look even cleverer, offer the person several packs from which to pick.
2. When you are given the selected card, balance it carefully on the outstretched index finger of your left hand. Then hand it back to the person, saying, 'Yes, I am able to spot that card again. I am remarkably sensitive to the weight of things.' Make sure that the card is face down throughout your performance.
3. The pack is now shuffled and the cards are given to you one by one. You weigh each on your finger as before, until at last the selected card is given to you. Immediately it rests across your fingers you exclaim, 'That's the card!' – and, sure enough, it is.

Secretly mark the chosen card with your thumbnail

How is it done? While you were weighing it the first time, you drew your thumbnail across a corner and that was the telltale clue for the second weighing.

THE FOUR JACKS

This is an easy trick to perform but one that is very effective, particularly if you can tell a good story. The four jacks are distributed throughout the pack, then magically reappear together on top.

1. The four jacks are taken from the pack and held up plainly in a fan for all to see. Behind these four cards, you hide four others. Having impressed on everybody that you are really showing them all the jacks and not kings or anything else, you place them on the top of the pack, which should be laid on the table in full view of everybody. So the four random cards are on the top, with the four jacks lying fourth to eighth.

Four random cards are hidden behind the fan of jacks

2. Now you start your story. 'Once upon a time, there were four burglars who entered a house and hid themselves in the attic. During the night, when everyone had gone to bed, one of them crept downstairs to the kitchen.' Take the top card – which the audience believes to be a jack – and place it at the bottom of the pack.

3. Continue: 'Then, the second burglar went silently down the stairs and entered the dining room on the second floor.' So saying, you slide the second card into the pack about three-quarters of the way down.

4. The story goes on: 'The third burglar thought it was time he did something, so off he went and crept into a bedroom on the second floor.' At this point you take the third card and put it into the pack about half-way down.

5. Continuing, you tell the audience about the fourth burglar. 'He set off to go downstairs,' you say, as you place the fourth card about a quarter of the way down the pack. The audience now believes that you have hidden all four jacks throughout the pack.

6. Then, you change your whole tone. 'Suddenly, the master of the house, realising that there were intruders, rang the alarm bell.' On saying this, you bang your fist on the pack. 'The burglars were so frightened that they all rushed back into the attic.' Then, slowly and deliberately, you turn over the top four cards of the pack and show that the jacks really have come back. Of course, when the four random cards were distributed through the pack, the jacks became numbers one to four.

THE NINE PIECES

You can apparently identify a segment of a card, even when blindfolded.

1. Ask a member of the audience to select any card from the pack, and then draw lines on it, as shown in the diagram, to divide the face of the card into nine sections. Number the pieces in pencil from 1 to 9, as shown.

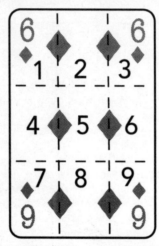

Divide the card into nine sections and number them

2. Next, carefully tear the card into the nine divisions indicated by the pencil lines. Place the pieces in a hat.
3. Ask another member of the audience to blindfold you, then to guide your hands to the hat.
4. Pick out the pieces one by one and tell the audience whether they are marked odd or even.

A glance at the diagram shows that, although the pieces are marked in order from 1 to 9, all the even-numbered sections have three torn sides and one straight cut side. No odd-numbered section has this. Therefore, by feeling, you can tell in a moment which is which.

OVER IT GOES

You can command the top card of a pack to turn over and reveal itself.

1. Ask a spectator to pick a card at random from the pack, to look at it and put it back on top of the pack.
2. Declare that you can make this chosen card reveal itself by the sheer force of your personality.
3. Hold a pack of cards, all face down, with the fingers at one of the short ends, the thumb at the other and the hand arched over the top. Without attracting the attention of the audience, slide the uppermost card of the pack to one side, so that it overhangs the others by about 2.5 cm (1 in).
4. Now hold the pack about 30 cm (12 in) above the table and drop it squarely on to the table, and as you do so, demand that the card shows its face. The pack lands with a thud and, sure enough, the top card has turned over. 'There it is!' you declare triumphantly.

The top card turns over

It is the pressure of the air that makes the overhanging card turn over. Once you have mastered this technique, you can work it into a variety of tricks.

THE SHOWER

You will have to work on your dexterity for this trick, but once mastered it is very effective. You will be able to throw the whole pack into the air and yet to pluck out two chosen cards.

1. Hand a pack of cards to a spectator. Ask him to shuffle the pack thoroughly and then to name a card.
2. Take the pack back, run through it and find the selected card. Hand it to the spectator with the remark, 'Is this the card?' On being assured that it is, place it on the top of the pack.
3. Now ask a second person to name another card. Find it and, after it has been confirmed as the chosen card, place it at the bottom of the pack.
4. Now you pretend to shuffle the pack, but what you actually do is to confine the shuffling to the central portion of the cards; the top and bottom cards stay in position.
5. Without attracting any attention, lick the thumb and index finger of your right hand. Grip the whole pack with them and at the same time slide the top and bottom cards a little off the pack, inwards towards your palm. Squeeze the pack to make the cards slide out of your grasp and, as they begin to fly, throw your hand upwards.

The effect is as though you have caught two flying cards

6. Up go the cards into the air and then they fall in a shower over your hand. When they lie scattered over the floor, two of them remain in your hand. They are the two cards selected by members of the audience.

The two chosen cards have remained in your hand because you licked your fingers; but, to the audience, it appears that while the cards were falling you were smart enough to single them out and catch them.

YOU KNOW THIS CARD

You can convince a friend that he knows more than he thinks he does, by the surreptitious application of simple logic.

1. Choose a card from the pack and put it face down on the table. You know what it is, but your friend has not seen it. In this example, let's say the card is the king of clubs. When you say to him, 'Of course, you know what card this is,' he will deny it. 'Oh yes, you do,' you say, 'I will prove to you that you do.' Then you proceed to question him.

2. First you ask, 'Do you prefer red or black cards?' If he replies red, you say, 'Right, that leaves the black cards.' Should he choose black, you say, 'Very good, I knew it.'

3. Next, ask, 'Now, of the black suits, which one is your favourite?' Again he can give two answers. If he favours clubs, you say, 'Of course,' and if he mentions spades you say, 'Good. That leaves clubs.'

4. Now you continue by asking whether he likes court cards or number cards. Should he choose court cards, you reply with the remark that most people do. However, should he seem perverse and vote for the number cards, you point out that that leaves the court cards.

By a process of elimination, you will end up with the correct card

5. Your next question is as to whether he prefers a male or female among the court cards. If he opts for female, nod your head and say that this doesn't surprise you; and continue by remarking that if he prefers female cards, that leaves the male cards. On the other hand, should he choose male, agree with him, saying, 'I could see you were a man's man!' or some such.

6. Lastly, you say, 'Of the male court cards, do you like the old or the young?' If he says old, you point out that this means the king, and you turn over the chosen card and show it is the king of clubs. Had he said he preferred the young, you would have pointed out that this left the king.

Any and every card in the pack may be singled out in exactly the same way – by a process of eliminating the unwanted cards. The curious thing about it all is that most people are very slow in understanding how they are made to choose the very card that is selected.

THOSE BOTTOM CARDS

With this trick you can successfully predict the bottom card of a cut. It relies on your being able to perform a false cut without hesitation, so practise until you can do it with really fluid movement.

1. Just before you do this trick, pick up the pack and memorise the four bottom cards, being absolutely sure of their order. Then attract the attention of your audience. Explain what the outcome of this trick will be.
2. Hold the pack lengthways in your left hand, faced down, with thumb on one long side and your fingertips on the other. Grip the pack with your right hand, with your fingers on top and your thumb below.
3. Casually, lick your thumb, then with your fingers slide off the cards, one or two at a time, towards your wrist, and tell your audience to stop you when they like.

Executing a false cut

4. As soon as they cry 'Stop!', announce that you will now cut the cards and that you can predict what the bottom card of the cut will be. Execute a false cut, so that as you draw off the cards comprising the cut, you slide with it the bottom card from the pack. Lift off the drawn-back cards and the lowest one is found to be exactly as you said.

Your thumb is slightly moistened so the bottom card is easy to pull back with a section of the main pack, as though you were really making a cut, and of course you know what this card is. You memorise four cards because you may be asked to repeat the trick – and if you can do so it adds to the mystery.

MAGNETISED TO YOUR HAND

Of course, you are not the ordinary type of person. For one thing, you possess magnetic properties rarely found in others. Naturally some people don't believe you when you tell them this, but it is a fact that if you clasp your left wrist with the right hand and stroke it gently, the palm of your left hand becomes alive with magnetic electricity. Of course it is understandable. The stroking generates static electricity, and there you are.

1. Telling your audience some sort of tall story such as this, you proceed to show that what you say is apparently perfectly true.
2. You do it this way. Take hold of a playing card with your left hand, with the fingers straight. Slip the card between them and the thumb. Hold out your hand, palm down, fingers pointing towards the audience. Then grip the wrist of this hand with the fingers of the right hand beneath, fingertips showing to the audience, with the card underneath. That done, gently move the right hand back and forth, as though supplying friction to the wrist.

The card is held by the index finger of your right hand

3. Everybody can see that you are supporting the card with the thumb of your left hand. Suddenly you look pleased and say, 'It's coming,' and then you stretch out the thumb and, if you like, the fingers. In fact, the index finger of your right hand is not round at the side with the other fingers. It is pressed against the palm of your left hand, with the card in between.

Everybody can see that it is quite impossible for you to be supporting the card, so, it must be the static electricity!

FINDING THE LADY

Amaze your friends when you can pick out the only queen from five cards.

1. Take the four kings and one queen from the pack and place them all face down on the table. Tell your audience that you can pick out the queen, even when the cards have been mixed up.
2. Ask one person to push the cards about on the table, while you turn away.
3. Turn back and stare intently at the cards for a moment, then point to the queen. Ask your chosen person to reveal that you are correct.

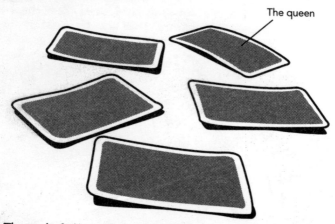

The queen

The curl of the cards is exaggerated here to show the effect

How is it done? Before dropping the cards on the table, you give the four kings a slight upward curl and the one queen an equally slight downward curl. That way, at a glance, you can see which are the kings because the ends of these cards don't lie quite flat and the centre of the queen rides up from the table. Of course, it spoils the trick if this curling process is overdone. It should be very slight and sufficient for only you to notice.

NAMING FOUR CARDS

This is a trick that works itself, as long as you deal out the cards correctly.

1. Take a pack of cards and let various people shuffle it. Then run off the four top cards. Ask a spectator to take them and remember one of them, forget all about the others and return the four to you.
2. Place the four cards face down on the table and deal off four more cards. Ask someone else to remember one of them, and proceed as before. Place the four cards on the top of the first four. Continue with two more sets of four cards and two more people.
3. When you have received sixteen cards in this way, deal them out face up, one card at a time, to give you four heaps of four. Deal one card to a heap at a time.

The first card chosen will be the last card of the heap indicated

4. Then ask the person to whom you first gave the cards to tell you in which heap his card now happens to be. Whichever heap he indicates, his card will be the last to be dealt of that heap.
5. In the case of the second, third and fourth people, their remembered cards will be the second, third and fourth cards from the top of the heaps they indicate.

Even if two people point to the same heap, the same rule applies.

25

THE SELECTED CARD

Just as in Naming Four Cards on page 25, this trick works itself, the solution being found in the position of the cards.

1. Take twenty-five cards and allow a friend to shuffle and cut them as they please. Then lay them out in the following order:

1	2	3	4	5
6	7	8	9	10
11	12	13	14	15
16	17	18	19	20
21	22	23	24	25

2. Having done that, ask an onlooker to think of any card in the layout and to tell you in which horizontal row it is now resting. Carefully note the left-hand card at the end of the row indicated.
3. Next, pick up the cards, but do it in this order. Take up card 1, place 6 on it and continue with 11, 16 and 21. Then follow 2, 7, 12, etc, to 25. As a card is lifted, be careful to place it on top of the others.
4. Now set out the cards once more in five horizontal rows. They will then take up these positions:

25	20	15	10	5
24	19	14	9	4
23	18	13	8	3
22	17	12	7	2
21	16	11	6	1

5. Once again ask the onlooker in which row the card he selected happens to be. When he tells you, look along the top or bottom row for the card that you noted at the left-hand

end of the row on the previous occasion. Above it or below it, vertically, in the row to which he now points, is the card he thought about.

For example, suppose 18 was the card thought about. The first time, your friend says, 'Row 4' and you look along to card 16. When the cards are relaid, he says 'Row 3'. You find card 16 and run up the vertical line until row 3 is reached. The card there is number 18.

THE KING OF HEARTS

'The king of hearts has always proved a very helpful card to me. It provides me with a kind of second sight.' When you correctly identify the top card of three stacks, your audience will think this must be true.

1. Hand an ordinary pack of cards to somebody and ask him to give it a good shuffle. When the pack is returned to you, say, half apologetically, 'Oh! But, of course, I want the king of hearts.' Rapidly run through the pack and throw out the king. While you sift through the cards you should also note the three top cards of the pack.
2. Place the whole pack, minus the king, on the table face downwards, and give it a good thump. The thump means nothing, but it makes people think that it has some mysterious effect.
3. Ask your volunteer to split the pack into three equal heaps as accurately as he can. Note which of these heaps comes from the top, because the three sighted cards will be in the heap.
4. Next, press down on each heap as though measuring its thickness. With an earnest expression, say, 'I need a few more cards here and one or two there.' As you say this, slide some cards from one heap to another and some more on to the third heap, ostensibly equalising the heaps but actually moving one of the three memorised cards on to the top of each heap.

Discreetly position the memorised cards

28

5. Now ask your volunteer to look at the top card of each pile and to remember it. Turn away while he does this.
6. Ask him to place the three piles in the form of a triangle and when he has done that you put the king of hearts on the top so that it lies on a portion of each top card.
7. Call upon the second sight that the king of hearts has given you and correctly announce the top three cards.

The equalising of the stacks must not be bungled or people will guess what you are doing. You must practise it until it can be done cleanly, so that you will appear perfectly honest.

THE SIX PACKS

Your friends won't be able to resist when you offer to show them a little X-ray reading.

1. Before you begin this trick make sure that you get a casual glance at the top card of a pack that is lying innocently on the table. Let's suppose it is the ace of hearts.
2. Ask somebody to cut the pack into six roughly equal heaps. Then announce to your audience that you can X-ray each of the six top cards.
3. You turn to the first heap – it may be any heap you like as long as it is not the original top of the pack. You look intently at the back of the card and, after a moment, say it is the ace of hearts, i.e. the top card of the pack (which, of course, it is not). You lift the card, look at the face, smile contentedly and say 'I was right.' However, you do not show it.
4. You now turn to the second heap and go through the same performance, but the card you name this time is the one taken from the previous heap.

Identify the card on the top of the second heap as the top card of the first heap

5. And so you go on from heap to heap, naming each card according to the one previously looked at. The only caution is that you must leave the heap that was originally on top of the pack until last.
6. The cards you announce are as follows:
   • For the first heap: the top card of the original pack
   • For the second heap: the top card of the first heap
   • For the third heap: the top card of the second heap
   • For the fourth heap: the top card of the third heap
   • For the fifth heap: the top card of the fourth heap
   • For the sixth heap: the top card of the fifth heap
7. As soon as you have completed the tour of the heaps, throw down the six cards triumphantly to show they are the ones you announced.

If anyone has kept a record of your calls, he will be able to check them against the cards.

THE FINGER POINTS

You are able to read the mind of one of your spectators, simply by watching him 'think' about his chosen card.

1. Offer a pack of cards to a spectator and invite him to shuffle them, and as he does so, to think of a card.
2. Take the pack back from him and spread it widely on the table with the faces up.
3. Take up a position a little way away from the spectator. Ask him to hold his right hand over the cards, with his index finger pointing downwards, and to move it slowly from one end of the row to the other and back again. Tell him that when he comes to his card he is to say mentally, 'That's it,' but that on no account must he hesitate or stop.
4. It is a psychological fact that if the spectator carries out your instructions he will hesitate for a fraction of a second when he comes to his card. This is quite obvious if you stand at a distance. At the very least, you should be able to say, to within five or six cards, where the chosen one lies.

Watch for a barely perceptible pause above the chosen card

5. Glance at the group of cards and remember their values; ignore the suits. As you return to the table to gather up the cards, cut the pack so that the group comes to the top and put it behind your back.

6. Ask the number of pips on the card and bring forward the correct one, face down. Now ask the suit and turn over the card.

If you struggle to remember the values on the cards, try thinking of them as a phone number: 246-783.

FIND THE QUEEN

When five cards are sealed into individual envelopes and then mixed, you are able to identify which is the only queen.

1. Take the four aces and one of the queens from an ordinary pack of cards. Make a show of inserting one card into each envelope, and then mixing them thoroughly.
2. What the audience doesn't know is that you place the aces into the envelopes on their sides. While it seems as though all five cards are inserted in this way, under the cover of the flap you actually turn the queen so that it is upright.

Turn the queen as you put it in the envelope

3. Now say that you will use the power of your mind to determine which envelope contains the queen. Hold them to your forehead one at a time and when you feel which envelope has the upright card in it, announce that you have found the queen.

Make sure that you camouflage the fact that you get your information by touch.

DETECTED BY FINGERPRINTS

Can it really be possible that you can tell which card was chosen, just by looking for fingerprints on it? Apparently so!

1. Ask a spectator to shuffle a pack of cards, and when he gives it back to you, sneak a look at the bottom card.
2. Turn your back and, holding the pack behind you, invite the spectator to make a free cut, then to take off the card on the lower section, look at it and remember it.
3. As he looks at it, turn to face him and explain that you are going to find his card by the fingerprints he leaves on it. Meanwhile, surreptitiously move the bottom card to the top of the portion left in your hand after the cut.

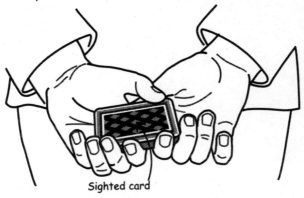

Sighted card

The chosen card is replaced on top of the one you know

4. Turn your back again, and ask the spectator to replace his card and then the portion he cut off, and to square the pack carefully.
5. Turn to face the audience and, under the pretence of looking for fingerprints, find the card you sighted. The chosen card is the one above it.

For an even better effect, you can ask your spectator to give the pack a short overhand shuffle, because there is very little chance of the two cards being separated.

Tricks that need some preparation

CUTTING THE ENVELOPE

It seems rather wonderful to produce an envelope, to put a playing card inside it, and then to cut the envelope in half across the middle – all without cutting the card. Yet you can do it with a little trickery.

1. First, make a slit down the middle of the envelope, from the top to the bottom.

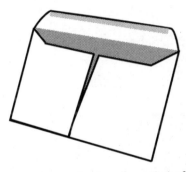

The first half of the cut is already made before the trick begins

2. Show the back of the envelope to the audience, holding the flap up with a finger that hides any part of the slit likely to show. Make a big show of inserting the card, which should reasonably fit the envelope, and stick down the flap in full view of everybody.
3. Then, take your scissors and get the lower tip into the slit, while the back of the envelope is facing away from the audience. Cut quickly across the envelope. Put down the scissors, slide the two halves of the envelope apart and show that the card is intact.

THE LOST ACE

This trick is so easy to do and yet it is such a complete swindle! The four aces are shown and then hidden in the pack. Yet when an unsuspecting audience member looks for them, one has disappeared.

1. Take the ace of diamonds out of the pack and hide it somewhere in the room, perhaps under the clock, before your audience arrives.
2. Take the aces of hearts, clubs and spades from the pack, together with the 3 of diamonds. Hold them in your hand as shown below in an irregular manner, so that it looks as though you hold all four aces. By covering the two outer spots on the 3 of diamonds you can give the impression that this card is the fourth ace.

How to position the four cards

3. Invite your audience to look carefully at your hand, while you point in turn to each card and identify it as an ace. 'Now, watch as I slip each one separately into the pack,' you say, as you very deliberately place the four cards into various parts of the pack.
4. Ask a member of the audience to shuffle the entire pack thoroughly. Then ask a second person to come forward and deal the cards with a view to recovering the four aces.

5. The person selected takes the pack, deals from one end to the other and finds only three aces. One has mysteriously disappeared!
6. Express surprise and then reveal the missing ace in whatever way you like.

THE INDEX CLUE

This trick is always fun to perform. It is such a dreadful swindle yet people rarely suspect how it is done.

1. You will need two packs of cards with identical backs. One pack is used as it is. On the second pack, cut away nine-tenths of the index corners and place the uncut tenth on top of the pack so that to all intents you have two identical, whole packs. Put an elastic band around the cut pack and hide it in your pocket.
2. Produce the sound pack of cards and hand it to someone in the audience. Invite that person to take a card, but to be absolutely sure that you cannot see it.
3. Ask for the return of all the other cards. As soon as you get them, slip a rubber band round the stack and put it in your pocket.
4. 'Now,' you exclaim in a serious way, 'I want everybody to see that card, and to that end I ask you to hold it well up in the air. So that there is no chance of me seeing it, I will turn my back.' Thereupon, you turn round and the card is held up for a few moments.
5. As you turn around, stuff your hands deep into your pockets. When you turn back, bring out the second, cut pack from your pocket.

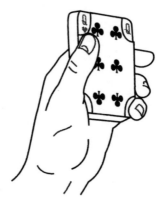

The chosen card is clearly visible

6. Remove the rubber band, and allow the cards to fall one after the other from your right to your left hand. As they are falling, the person with the card slips it back into the pack, anywhere. Take care that the cut corners remain hidden. Remind your audience that you cannot possibly know where it has gone and, as you did not see it while it was being shown round, you cannot possibly tell what it was.

7. Hold the pack tightly and at arm's length, with their backs to the audience. 'Was it a court card or merely a numeral card?' you enquire. On being given the answer, you immediately announce the name of the hidden card. Of course, the telltale corner of the chosen card sticks out beyond those that have been clipped.

THE 'ONE-WAY' CARD TRICK

Have you noticed that most of the number cards have a right and a wrong way up, though the court cards and a few others are both ends alike? For this trick, you use only the asymmetrical cards. Before you begin, take out all the symmetrical number cards but leave the court cards in.

1. Tell the audience that this trick requires a tremendous amount of memorising and, were you to use a full pack, it would probably result in a fearful headache. Therefore, with their kind permission, you propose to use only about half the pack. Accordingly, you throw out all the court cards and declare that those that are left will do nicely.

2. Ask someone in the audience to shuffle the cards and then ask her to pick any card she likes, to look at it and then return it to the pack anywhere she chooses. While she looks at the card, hold the rest of the pack in your hands with the long side towards your body. When you invite your victim to return the card to the pack, it is a simple matter to turn the pack whichever way is necessary to ensure that the card is returned in the opposite orientation.

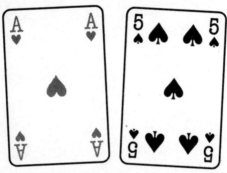

Two of the cards that clearly have a 'right' and 'wrong' way up

3. Invite your chosen person to shuffle the pack. Remind the audience that it is hopeless to expect you to know where the chosen card lies within the pack and, equally of course, you have not seen the card, though everybody in the crowd has.

4. Affect an air of concentration as you try to 'remember' which card was chosen, then suddenly smile as though the mystery has cleared up. Deal out the cards one by one, face up. You will be able to see which card has been inverted and, on reaching it, point it out as you exclaim, 'There it is!' to the astonishment of the audience.

By rejecting the court cards in front of the audience, they will not suspect that you have already shortened the pack. Of course, all the shuffling in the world will not reverse the cards.

THE FAKED HALF-DOZEN

How can a chosen card be in two places at once? It's easy – if you know how to cheat! You will need an ordinary pack of cards and six extra cards of exactly the same size. Fairly thick ones are best. Take the six extras and the six that correspond to them from the pack. You can use any cards, but choose six that are easy to remember. Split these twelve cards so that the backs and fronts are separated. Throw away the backs, then stick the twelve fronts together in pairs to make six faked cards. Make sure that in no case are the back and front the same.

The jack of hearts on one side but the 7 on the other

1. Present your audience with what is apparently a perfectly ordinary pack of cards, and hold up six of them (the faked cards) with their faces towards the audience. 'Now, my friends,' you say in a cheery way, 'what are these cards? Ah, yes, the king, queen, jack, 10, 9 and 8 of hearts [or whatever]. Will somebody be good enough to name any one of these cards?' Someone will call out, for instance, the queen. 'Very well then,' you continue, 'it shall be the queen.'
2. Take the queen (or whichever card is selected) and place it in a box. Make sure that everybody sees that it is the queen that goes into the box, then close the box, ask someone to shake the box and listen to the card rattling inside.

3. Place a silk handkerchief over the five remaining cards and indulge in a few moments' patter, as though you are waiting for something to happen. For example, make some remark about the lady exercising her prerogative to keep people waiting.
4. However, when a few moments have elapsed, ask someone to rattle the box again and, on being told that the card is still inside, whip the handkerchief off the cards and pick up the queen from among them.

The secret of success lies in indulging in some amusing patter at the very moment when the weakest part of the performance is happening. Don't allow people to handle the cards. When you hold up the faked six, hold them squarely; people should not see behind them. When the trick is finished, get on to the next piece of business without any hesitation.

THE BOWLER-HAT TRICK

Your audience puts little pieces of card into a bowler hat. Somehow you are able to pull out a piece bearing whatever pip is requested. How? It's all in the preparation. Take a bowler hat and turn up the inner band. Squeeze the silk band on the outside out of position and cut a small hole in the felt behind the band.

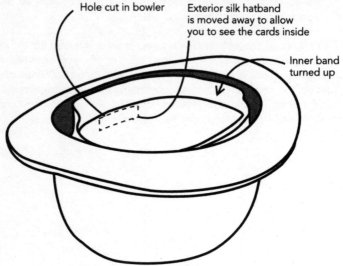

Hole cut in bowler

Exterior silk hatband is moved away to allow you to see the cards inside

Inner band turned up

You can easily see what is in the hat

1. Take six odd cards from an old pack and hand them to the audience. Ask those concerned to tear pieces out of the cards, so that there is one complete pip on each section of card. For obscure reason, most people love doing this; perhaps it the sense of destruction that provides the enjoyment!

2. When that part of the performance has been completed and you have commented on the zest that the people have shown in tearing up your cards, pass round the prepared bowler hat for examination. Don't let the audience look too closely at the hat: just enough to see that it is an ordinary bowler, quite unaltered.

3. Next, get someone to put all the pip pieces in the hat, mix them up and hand the hat to you.
4. You take the hat and hold it high up, in front of you. Then you reach up with your right hand and stir the pips. So that there is no possibility of you seeing inside the bowler, you turn up the leather band inside. It now stands up like a wall all round the inner edge.
5. 'Now,' you say, pointing to somebody, 'what would you like? A heart, a diamond, a spade or a club?' The person says 'a club', and straightaway you draw a club out of the magic hat. You do this about six times and, on each occasion, you bring out the pip required.

Of course, with the hat high up in front of you – on your eye level, in fact – you discreetly lift the band with your thumb and simply peep through the hole to select the right piece of card.

THE FOUR DIAMONDS

An unsuspecting member of the audience gives you individual pips from a cut card. Yet you always seem to have one more than you should have. Before you begin this trick, you should cut up an old diamonds card so that you have a selection of single pips concealed in your left-hand pocket.

1. Give someone a card with four or more diamonds on it, and a pair of scissors. Ask them to cut out four of the pips to shape. The audience usually finds this hugely entertaining, so they will not notice that you are now standing with your hands in your pockets. Manipulate one of the concealed pips so that it rests between the little finger and third finger of your left hand.

The extra pip ready to be added to those in your hand

2. When the pips have been cut, show that your left hand is empty. For this, you display it opened out flat.
3. Ask the individual to hand you the pips one at a time. Take each pip with your right-hand index finger and thumb and put it in your left hand, which you open and close as each pip goes into it. Count aloud as they go into the left hand – one, two, three – and, when the fourth pip is given to you, flick it into the air and let it fall to the ground. 'No, I won't have that one,' you say. 'It hasn't been cut properly.'

4. So, of course, you only have three pips in the left hand. But on opening it, there are four to be seen. The explanation is that when the first pip was placed in your hand you also transferred the hidden pip.

There is no reason why you should not repeat this trick, if you have come prepared with several diamonds in your pocket. On a second performance, do not reject the fourth pip, but flick away the second or third.

THE DUMMY EAR

Before the eyes of your audience you turn an 8 into a 2. The lengthy preparation of the prop for this trick is well worth the effort. You will need to spoil a card for this, so if you have an old, incomplete set, use that, rather than ruining a new pack.

- Take any one of the cards, but preferably a 5, 6, 7, 8, 9 or 10. Then cut off one of the corners, making it large enough to include the corner index and one of the adjacent spots or pips.
- Gum a hinge of paper along the top and side edge, but not along the cut edge.
- Following that, cut another card to exactly the same shape as the first and fix it to the gummed hinge as shown in the diagram. You now have a triangular pocket, with a portion of a numeral card on the front and a piece of pattern on the back.
- Now, get three, or perhaps four, cards with the backs bearing the same pattern as found on the rear side of the triangular pocket. To be on the safe side, see that the pocket will fit snugly on the corners of the cards.
- Take three or four cards, one of which should be an ace or a 2. Let's assume here that you use the 2. Slip the ear or triangular pocket on one of its corners and place it, in a fan, with the other cards. It will not look like a 2 now, but rather an 8 (or whatever was selected at the outset). The part not covered by the ear is masked by the fan formation of the other cards. You are now ready to perform the trick.

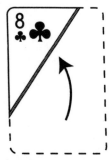

The ear for slipping on to other cards

1. Show the audience the fan, holding the cards at the bottom edges, and tell them that their eyes are not quick enough to follow your movements. Say that you are going to challenge them to pick out the 8 when you place the cards on the table.

2. Everybody stares hard and you transfer the cards from one hand to the other. You are now gripping the top edges, whereas just now you were holding the bottom edges. In transferring the cards from one hand to the other, you also turn them over, so that the backs are now uppermost. You do no shuffling and you do not quite close the fan.

3. One by one, you place the cards, backs up, on the table, and you do not put them out in a row. The idea is to pretend there is some mystery in the way you are laying them, when of course, there is not.

4. On coming to the card with the ear, you deftly slide the card out of your hand and leave the ear in it, and so the '8' reverts to a 2.

5. As soon as all the cards are on the table, everybody points triumphantly to the 8. Then you turn it over - it is not an 8, but the 2.

SIXES AND SEVENS

People are not very observant, and this fact may be made use of in the following trick, in which you apparently make two cards come together in the centre of a pack. Before you begin, place the 6 of spades and 7 of clubs next to each other in the middle of the pack.

1. Take the prepared pack and, with your friend looking on, run through it and hand out the 6 of clubs and 7 of spades. Hand the two cards to him and, with the pack squared up on the table, cut it twice. Get your friend to insert one of the cards in each cut. It will be advisable to make one of the cuts low down in the pack and the other high up. In other words, they should be far apart.

The two original cards are forgotten as the two near-matches are shown to be together

2. Now, give the pack two resounding blows and pick it up. Then, run through it, turning each card as you go. When you reach about half-way through, what do you find? The 6 of spades and 7 of clubs next to each other – yet the two cards were placed far apart in the pack. Amazing!

Of course, the cards that your friend inserted were not these at all: they were the 6 of clubs and the 7 of spades. Not one person in a hundred will notice the deception.

MOVING CARDS

You are able to tell your friends how many times they have moved cards – and produce a card of the correct number to confirm it.

1. Before you begin this trick you will need to have separated the ace to jack of one suit from a pack and laid them in a line without drawing attention to yourself. Arrange eleven cards in a row on the table, all face down, beginning with a jack and continuing down to an ace, as follows:

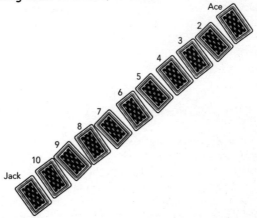

2. Now, tell your friends that if, while you are out of the room, they will move as many cards as they like from the right-hand end of the row to the left-hand end, when you return you will pick up a card that indicates the number of cards they have moved. For instance, if they move three cards, you will turn over a 3 and if they move five, you will turn over a 5.
3. There is just one proviso: they may only move one card at a time, though they may move as many as they like before you return.
4. When they have moved whatever number of cards they have decided on, you return to the room, look intently at the cards as though making some mental calculation and then turn the card on the extreme left. This indicates the number of cards moved – always.

THE PENCIL LINE

A selected card is hidden within a pack, yet you are able to identify it at a moment's notice. Before you begin, take a pack of cards that has been handled a fair amount and draw a light pencil line across one side of the pack, about 2.5 cm (1 in) from one of the short ends.

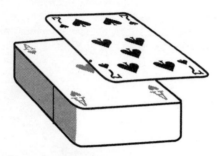

The dot on the edge of the card will give it away

1. In an unconcerned way, drop the prepared pack on the table and ask someone to pick out a card without you seeing it.
2. When that has been done, explain what you want done next, and as you do so, turn the pack round. Say that you would like the card to be returned to the pack. Stand back from the table while this is being done, so that there can be no suspicion about the performance.
3. Then comes the climax. You run through the pack and throw out the selected card. It is all quite easy. The card, when returned, has a pencilled dot showing up plainly on it. The dot is the card's contribution to the line, misplaced.

You need to use an old pack, because on a new pack the pencil line would show up too much. A glance at the pack is all that is necessary to locate the dot – but don't try this trick if you are shortsighted!

THE ROSETTE OF CARDS

A rosette of cards magically sticks to your upturned hand. You will need two loops of light-coloured hair. One is slipped from side to side across the wide part of your hand and the other goes from between your third and little fingers to the wrist at the root of the thumb.

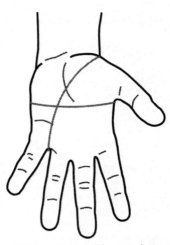

The loops of hair will hold the cards in position

1. Hand someone a pack of cards and ask them to pick out any nine cards for you.
2. Place one of them flat on the palm of your left hand and then arrange the remaining eight so that they lie partly under the first card and partly under themselves. You thus form a kind of rosette on your hand. What you actually do is to slide the cards under the loops.
3. Now clap your right hand over the cards, press down tightly and then reverse the position of your hands, while keeping them firmly together.
4. Now, slowly take away the right hand – it is underneath – and amazingly the cards do not fall.

The hair cannot be seen.

SEVEN ANY WAY

As your friend concentrates hard on one of three heaps of cards, you can tell him which heap he has in mind. Before you begin, arrange the heaps as follows:

- One heap contains seven cards
- The second heap includes the four 7s
- The third heap is made up of an ace, a 2 and a 4

Each of the groups can be defined as a 'seven' heap

1. Arrange the three heaps of cards in front of your friend and ask him to concentrate hard on one of them.
2. You glance at him with a serious expression that makes the onlookers think you are really reading his mind. Then you scribble something on a piece of paper.
3. 'Very good,' you say. 'Which is the heap?' The friend points to one of them, and you ask him to read what is written on the paper. It says, 'You will choose the seven heap.'
4. 'Now turn over your heap,' you say. The person turns over his heap and, sure enough, it is a seven heap. You are perfectly correct and, the trick being finished, you quickly gather up the cards.

Of course, whichever heap was chosen it would answer to the description of a seven heap and fit your written prediction.

ODD OR EVEN

Show how you can tell if a portion of cards contains an odd or even number. Before you start, arrange a complete pack in red, black, red, black sequence. Have the values scattered so that no attention will be paid to the arrangement.

Arrange the cards alternately red and black

1. Ask someone to cut the pack into two portions and tell your audience that you can judge by the feel whether each section contains an odd or even number of cards.
2. Naturally, you have to feel the cards to get an idea of their thickness. While you are doing this, get a glimpse of the bottom card of each portion.
3. If the bottom card of the two portions is the same colour, the portions both contain an even number of cards; if the bottom cards are not the same colour, the portions both contain an odd number of cards. Make your announcement with a flourish.

As long as you glimpse the cards without being detected, this trick cannot fail.

Working with an accomplice

GUESSING THE ACES

With the aid of your accomplice, you demonstrate the ability to detect whenever an ace is dealt. Make sure you are sitting next to your co-conspirator.

1. Tell your friends as they sit round the table that, if someone will deal the cards, you can distinguish when an ace is turned. It is because aces have a peculiar attraction for you and that, though you do not fully understand it, you are conscious of the effects.
2. So you consent to being blindfolded and whenever the dealer turns an ace you mention the fact, to the amazement of the onlookers.
3. Your accomplice watches the cards, and as soon as an ace comes up she presses her foot against yours.

Subtle footwork signals the turn of the ace

If you end up separated from your accomplice, she may have to resort to discreet throat-clearing, but this is not as easy to do.

THE TWO TOGETHER

Many impossible things become possible when working with an accomplice, and here is one of them. You can apparently control two cards so that they lie together in the pack. Before you begin, agree with your accomplice which card he will select, and place this card at the bottom of the pack.

1. You get out a pack of cards and ask two people to think of any card they like. You already know that your accomplice is going to say the 3 of diamonds (or whatever).
2. When the two people have named their cards for all to hear, you say, 'Very well, I will bring those cards together,' and you give the pack a bang with your fist.

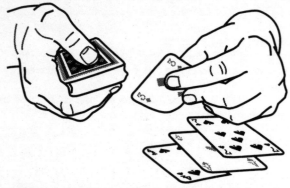

A false deal will bring the two named cards together

3. Now the fun begins. You deal the cards, one by one, from the bottom of the pack, but before doing so, draw the 3 of diamonds about 2.5 cm (1 in) back into the palm of your hand. Here it is out of the way while you are dealing the other cards.
4. As soon as the card belonging to the innocent party comes along, you say, 'Now for the 3 of diamonds,' and sure enough that is the next card.

You merely squeezed your palm and forced the card back into position, where it is waiting to be dealt in the ordinary way.

CODES AND CONFEDERATES

Demonstrate your psychic ability by announcing the name of a card chosen from a pack, even though you cannot possibly know what it is. With the aid of your accomplice and a secret code, anything is possible. Without a doubt, an accomplice is of greatest use to you when you have both memorised a carefully compiled code of your own. Here is the framework of such a code.

1. First, when he openly poses as your assistant, he can frame a question that, by means of your code, lets you know the details of the card. He asks you about the card, perhaps, by using a sentence containing as many words as there are pips on the card. Thus, 'What is it?' would be a 3 of one of the suits. The first word of his question gives the clue to the suit. Thus, 'what' may be hearts, 'which' clubs, and so on. Special arrangements will be needed for aces and 2s, because one and two-word sentences are apt to cause suspicion.

A click of the pen – that means hearts

2. Second, when your friend is not known to be connected with your operations, he can give you all the information you require by the way he handles a pen, for instance. To click the end means hearts; to scratch his head with it, clubs, etc. Or he may move his head about, touch certain parts of his face, cough, get out his handkerchief and so on.

It is not in the best interests of a conjuror that a complete code should be given here, since it is far better that he should frame his own. Then nobody but he and his accomplice will understand it. Of course, no code is of any value unless it has been practised and made perfect.

CARD TELEPATHY

You send your assistant out of the room, yet when she returns she knows which card has been selected.

1. Introduce your assistant to the audience and build up her incredible psychic powers. Have a member of the audience escort her out of the room.
2. Now offer a pack of cards to a spectator and ask him to make a free selection of any card, show it to everyone and then put it in his pocket. You, too, should make a mental note of what the card is, but don't make a show of doing so.
3. Insert a blank slip of paper into a plain envelope with an ordinary wooden pencil. Ask another spectator to take this to your assistant and return with a message from her.

Left side, first letter – that means the ace of clubs

4. As in Codes and Confederates on page 61, you can tell your assistant all she needs to know by using your own secret language. For instance, if the card is a heart, stick down only the right side of the envelope; a club, stick down the left; a diamond, just the tip; a spade, the whole flap. Similarly, the value of the card is indicated by using your fingernail to mark the pencil next to the letters of the trade name. For example, if the card is an ace, put a mark next to the first letter.

As before, it is best to devise your own code for this trick.

CARD X

Your assistant must be very gifted, because she can tell what card is being held, even with its back to her – and while wearing a blindfold.

1. Invite a spectator to shuffle a pack of cards thoroughly and then return it to you.
2. Introduce your assistant and say that she will act as medium. Ask her to sit on a stool and place a blindfold over her eyes. As you adjust this, add eight or ten cards previously memorised to the pack you still hold in your hand. They should have been hidden either in the folds of the lady's clothing or, perhaps, in a hidden pocket under the seat of the stool. The exact location will depend on the circumstances in which you are performing the trick.

Palm the memorised cards on to the top of the pack

3. Now take the cards one at a time and hold them so that the audience can see their faces clearly. With much theatricality, your assistant will name them. The air of mystery can be enhanced if your assistant hesitates or makes slight mistakes and corrections as she identifies the cards.

Tricks with special packs

For the tricks in this chapter, a little more preparation of your pack is required before you start working on the tricks. You can also buy special decks – such as a deck of identical cards – from magic stores.

THE FAKED PACK

Your unsuspecting audience member picks a card and returns it to the pack. Despite a thorough shuffling of the pack, you are able to identify the chosen card. For this you will need two packs with identical backs. One of these is a regular pack; the other comprises fifty-two identical cards. You will also need a table to work behind.

1. Run out the pack of identical cards in a fan formation, backs towards the audience, and ask someone to come forward and select one from your hand. He thinks he is being given a free choice; you, of course, know different!
2. As soon as the person has picked one, close up the pack and get him to replace the card anywhere among the others. Then, in front of everybody, give them a good shuffle as you return to your table.

Not much of a choice – the cards are all the same

3. This is where your patter comes in. You must keep the audience entertained with your witty repartee, so that everyone is distracted as you swap the fake pack for the regular one. How you do this depends on your dexterity. You might have the second pack in your pocket or resting on the table with a selection of props.
4. Now deal out the cards face up, one by one. As soon as you reach the card that was 'selected', you point it out.

This is not an easy trick as it depends on a skilful touch with the cards. On no account repeat the trick: the result would be disastrous!

THE HOLY CARDS

A card selected by a member of your audience slides out of a pack, as if by magic. You will need a pack of fifty-two identical cards and about twelve cards from a regular pack with the same back design. Cut a hole of about 4 cm (1½ in) square in the centre of these regular cards and place them on your table under a card with the same back and face as those in the identical pack. This portion should be concealed either on your table or in your pocket, whichever you find easier.

1. Hold out the pack of (identical) cards in a fan, face downwards, and ask someone to select a card, look at it and remember it, but not let you know what it is.
2. Offer them the fan and invite them to replace the card anywhere they like. Give the pack a thorough shuffle.
3. Return to your table and under the cover of some entertaining patter, square the cards on the table and at the same time place them on top of the prepared portion without drawing attention to it.
4. Now come forward towards your audience and tell them that you are going to make the selected card slide out of the pack, although you do not know what it is.

From underneath you can put your finger through the hole to slide out the chosen card

5. Hold the pack, face upwards, so that it is lying almost in the palm of your right hand. You have previously licked the tip of the third finger. This finger is tucked below the pack. It reaches up, through the cut-out portion, to the first complete card. By drawing your finger along this card it slides out of the pack. Ask your volunteer to name his chosen card and, sure enough, it is the sliding card.

Like The Faked Pack on page 66, this trick depends on you being able to divert the audience's attention while you manipulate the cards. Practise until you have it perfect.

THE ENCYCLOPEDIA

How can it be that a card picked at random can be identified by examining the pages of an encyclopedia into which it is pushed? Easily, when you use a pack of fifty-two identical cards and a thick book. Before you begin, position one of the identical cards so that it protrudes slightly from one of the short ends of the book, at a position to suit the directions given below.

1. Ask a member of the audience to come out and give you a hand. Take out the pack of (identical) cards, shuffle them and then fan them. Ask your volunteer to select one, to look at it and show it to the other onlookers but not to let you see it.
2. Now you produce the book and, offering one of the short ends to your assistant, request that he forces the card not quite all the way into the book, anywhere he likes.
3. Now say that you need a second volunteer. While you are choosing someone else to carry on the trick, you pull out the card and slip it into your pocket, or if you do not feel capable of doing this, you push it completely into the book to hide it. Then you turn the book round and show the card that you previously put in. Thus both ends of the book are used, but you must not let this fact become obvious.

Card sticking out of the book

4. Turn to your second assistant and say, 'You see where the card is sticking out? Please open the book at the place indicated by the card.' When the person has done so, you remark, 'It is page 90 and 91, I believe.' They look up in amazement, because you are perfectly correct. You then proceed, 'What is the third word on the second line of page 91?' They hunt for the word and you say, 'Black'. 'That,' you say, 'describes the colour of the card.' Then you go on to remark that the initial letters of the fifth, seventeenth, tenth, eleventh and twenty-first lines spell the word 'Spade', and you say that spades is the suit of the card chosen at the outset.

5. As a final show of mystery, you ask your helper to count the words on the eighteenth line. 'There are five,' you add, 'and it was the 5 of spades that was chosen.' Everything you say is absolutely correct.

You know the name of the card that will be selected, so all you have to do is remember the details of the clues.

CARD TURNOVER

A selected card is returned to a pack that is shuffled. When the cards are fanned, the chosen one has mysteriously turned over, not once but twice. This trick is simplicity itself – as long as you have a pack of cards that are double-backed. Choose a pack with backs that match those of a conventional pack for this trick and make up a fake pack consisting of twenty-six ordinary cards and below them twenty-six double-backed cards.

1. Ask a spectator to choose any card, but make sure he picks one of the ordinary ones from the top half of your pack. Ask him to look at it and remember it and then have him it return it to the bottom half, that is, amongst the double-backed cards. A little judicious fanning will direct the card to the right half of the pack.

The choice must be made from the conventional cards in the top half of the pack

2. Square up the cards and in doing so turn the pack over. Utter some magic spell that orders the chosen card to turn over.
3. Spread almost half the cards on the table before you, and the chosen card will be revealed face up among apparently face-down cards.

4. Pick up the card and insert it in the lower half of the pack, face down, that is, among the ordinary cards that are face up. Again, turn the pack over without drawing attention to it and order the card to repeat its somersault.
5. Spread the cards on the table and the selected card appears face up in the face-down pack.

Take care not to expose the 'wrong' half of the pack when you spread the cards.

THREE HIDDEN CARDS

To the amazement of your audience you can instantly withdraw three chosen cards from a shuffled pack. All you need to do this is a shaved, or stripper, pack. This is well-known device amongst conjurors, but if worked sparingly and with finesse it can be used to great effect. To make such a pack:

- Carefully pile the fifty-two cards exactly one above each other.
- With a ruler and a sharp knife, cut a thin strip off both of the long edges so that the cards taper, that is, they are slightly wider at one end than the other.
- If the cutting is done cleanly and not too generously, nobody will notice that the pack has been tampered with in any way.

The slight taper will be easily detectable by your touch

1. Now for a way of using the cards in a trick. Ask someone to draw a card from the pack and put it back, all without letting you see it. Then you ask someone else to do the same, likewise a third person. As the first card is returned, surreptitiously turn the pack so that it ends up in the opposite orientation to the bulk of the cards. Turn the pack back to its original position for the second and third selections.

2. When the three cards are back in the pack, give them a good shuffle, then say, 'Now for the three cards.' Instantaneously you draw your fingers and thumb along the side edges of the pack and the three chosen cards slide out.

When you start this trick, the cards are all arranged one way in the pack – short ends one way, long ends the other. But when the three cards are returned to the pack, they lie the opposite way to the rest of the pack. Thus they stand out at one end and that enables you to slide them out.

ANY CARD YOU LIKE

A casual glance at the back of a card will enable you to tell your audience the name of that card. You will need cards with a special pattern on the back for this trick, that is, decorated with a pattern of tiny squares, all within a surrounding frame. Think of the first row of squares as hearts, the second as clubs, the third as diamonds and the fourth as spades. Then, according to the suit of the card, place a tiny dot in the square representing its face number, counting from the left. Thus a dot in the third square on the second row tells you you're dealing with the 3 of clubs.

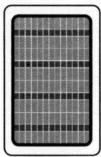

The dot indicates the 3 of clubs

To save a great deal of counting in the case of the higher numbered cards, such as 10 and the court cards, put a dot on the line dividing the seventh and eighth squares. Then for these you will only have to count on from seven.

1. Invite a member of the audience to shuffle the pack and then, holding it in your right hand, allow the cards to fall slowly face down from your hand on to the table. Ask the spectator to call out, 'Stop' at any time he likes.
2. You stop and with a casual look at the back of the last card to fall – and at the dots you marked – you are able to name it.

Do not use new cards – soiled ones obscure the marks more – and make the marks in the same coloured ink as the design. Count jacks as eleven, queens as twelve and kings as thirteen.

ROYAL QUARREL

Like Three Hidden Cards on page 74, you will need a stripper pack for this trick. Then it is a simple matter to reunite the king and queen, despite their separation within a pack and thorough shuffling.

1. Tell the audience that, much to your regret, the king and queen of hearts in the pack you are holding have had a terrible row. With the help of some of your friends around, you propose to bring the two antagonists together.
2. Having given them this story, you hand the queen to someone and ask them to put it back in the pack anywhere they like while you drop the cards from one hand to the other. Repeat this with another person, using the king. Offer the pack to them so that they are made to put the short ends of their cards with the long ends of the cards in the pack.

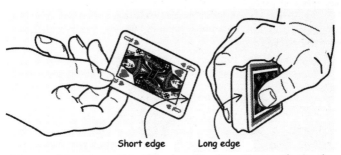

Short edge   Long edge

The card is returned in the opposite direction to the pack

3. Shuffle the whole pack vigorously and then, suddenly, you run your hands apart and hold up the king and queen together. Hold the long end of the pack in your left hand and slide your right hand along the edges so that the reversed cards can be drawn out.

With a little practice, the separating can be done so quickly that nobody can see what was actually done.

77

YOU CAN'T DO AS I DO

Despite his best intentions, your poor victim can't end up with the same hand of cards as you do – but then he doesn't have a double-faced card like you! Before you begin, arrange the cards so that, with the pack face up, the seventh one is actually a double-faced card.

1. Invite a member of the audience to join you, then peel off the top five cards from your prepared pack and give them to him in a fan, face up. Take the next five cards for yourself. Your fan will have the double-faced card placed second from the right.
2. Ask the spectator to do exactly as you do. Close the cards together, face up. Put the top card on the bottom of the packet, face down. Move the top card to the bottom, face up. Move the top card to the bottom, face down.
3. Spread your cards and show three cards face up, two cards backs up. The spectator spreads his and they are in the same position. Compliment him on his dexterity and close up the packets again.
4. Now place the top card on the bottom, face down. Turn the top card face down. Turn the cards over and spread them.

One of your volunteer's cards will be the wrong way up

5. This time yours are all face up, but the unsuspecting spectator has one card face down!

Once the cards are arranged correctly this trick works itself.

THE THICK CARD

Despite cutting and shuffling a pack, you are able to deal the cards to find that chosen by a spectator. This is because you are using a fake card that you have created by sticking two together.

- Take any court card you like from a disused pack. Cut the white edges from the picture area and stick the latter on to a corresponding card of a serviceable pack. If you do the work well, nobody will notice that there is anything amiss with the card or the pack.

Stick the smaller inside portion on to the whole card to make a thicker, fake card

- When the sticking is finished, mix this thick card with the others and cut the pack. You will find that the cut can always be made so that the thick card comes at the top of the cut. This is, of course, a secret that can be put to excellent use.

1. Ask a member of the audience to choose a card, to show it to the other people watching, but to make sure that you cannot see it.
2. Cut the pack into two sections. Invite your spectator to put the card on to the top of the cut, and then close up the pack.
3. Shuffle the cards away from the cut, then deal off the cards, one by one. When you reach the selected card, announce its name with a flourish and have it confirmed by the audience.

The chosen card is, of course, the one above the thick card. This is because your cut came at the thick card.

Tricks with technical props

As you become more proficient at basic, impromptu card tricks, you might want to venture into more of a performance by incorporating into your act a few that require the use of technical props. The tricks that follow show you how to make a few devices that will add an extra dimension to your show, and give examples of how they can be used.

THE FLYING CARD

Can cards fly? The answer is yes, when you have acquired the mysterious power to make them – and, of course, you have the right props.

- You need two identical packs of cards, one of which must be modified as follows. Split it into two roughly equal portions and stick the cards together, so that you end up with two 'blocks'.
- Take a piece of very thin sewing thread 20 cm (8 in) long and stick it about 1 cm ('/₂ in) from the end of the face of the bottom card of one of the blocks, and lie it along the length of the card. Hold the thread in place with your finger and loop it back up the card again.
- Now place the second block underneath, as shown. You will need to hold the loose end in your right hand to make the card fly in the following trick.

Block of cards stuck together

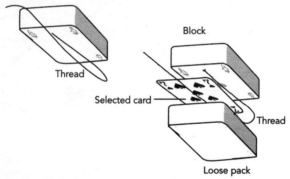

Block

Thread

Selected card

Thread

Loose pack

As you pull the thread it forces the card out into the room

1. Take the genuine pack of cards and play with it for a moment or two, while you tell your audience about the marvellous ability you have developed that enables you to command a card to fly. Ask someone to name any card they like. Let's suppose they pick the ace of clubs. 'Very well,' you say, 'the ace of clubs it is.' Run through the pack and bring it out.

2. Now go behind your table, which you have positioned a little way from the audience. Lean with both hands on the table for a fraction of a second while you ask everybody to watch carefully. Slowly and deliberately slide the ace of clubs into any part of the pack at one of the short ends of the pack. What you actually do, of course, is to slide the card into the false pack, which you switch during the brief time you are touching the table, so that the card is held inside the loop of thread.

3. 'Now,' you say, 'I am going to see if the ace of clubs will do as I command.' Bring the pack up to your eye level, in front of your face. Rest it in the palm of your left hand, with a finger and thumb spread up either side. Steady the pack with your right hand at the back.

4. With a mystical tone, you say, 'Ace of clubs, fly, fly.' In one swift movement, raise your hands upwards and at the same time pull on the thread. The ace of clubs apparently jumps out of the pack, soars up into the air and falls to the ground.

When the selected card is forced into the slot, the thread grips it on both faces, and when the flying is about to take place, all that is necessary is a smart pull on the free end.

THE BALANCING BALL

Wouldn't it be impressive if you could make the ball run along the edge of a hand of cards? As a matter of fact, you can!

- You will need a solid rubber ball, just a bit smaller than a golf ball. Make a small hole in it.
- Take a piece of thin but stiff wire and make a loop at one end that will fit over the tip of your thumb.
- The other end should be bent into a right angle and then inserted into the small hole.

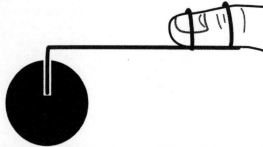

The wire support holds the ball behind the fan of cards

1   Remark to your audience that you seem to have the uncanny knack of being able to balance a ball on the edge of a playing card.
2. With this you pick up about twelve cards and make them into a neat, regular fan with no angular dips between the cards. At the same time discreetly put the wire support on your thumb. Hold the fan with your fingers facing the audience and thumb supporting it at the back. Now pick up the ball and stand it on the edge of your fan of cards. Bring your wire support into position so that it goes up behind the cards with the horizontal arm pointing forwards. Press the ball on to the wire, using the pre-made hole.

3. If you now waggle your thumb, the ball is made to look as though it were running along the edges of the cards and, if you are careful to twist the fan slightly when the ball seems to want to run downhill, the illusion will be complete.

Do not have any pattern on the ball, as this will spoil the illusion that it is rolling.

CUTTING THE MATCHBOX

This neat trick requires a nifty device to work the illusion.

- Take two playing cards, a court card and one other, and cut a rectangle from each so that they are like the shape marked A in the diagram opposite. The portion removed must in each case be slightly larger than the width and depth of an ordinary matchbox.
- The two pieces have to be fitted together along the north, south and west edges, but the east edge is open and so the two cards, when joined, form a pocket. Use double-sided sticky tape for this.
- But before the two cards are put together, two loops of elastic must be fitted inside the pocket. One loop starts at the point indicated by the upper cross and travels inwards, parallel to the dotted line, a little further than where the cut-out section ends, and then returns to the cross. One end of the elastic is fitted to the upper inner face of the pocket and the other to the lower inner face. The second loop takes up a corresponding position, but starts from the lower cross in the diagram.
- When the pocket is made, it should have two inside loops that cannot be seen and one of its surfaces should represent the back of an ordinary card. The other surface should represent any one of the court cards.
- In addition to the pocket, a loose piece of card is needed. One face of it should match the back of the pocket and the other the court card figuring on the pocket. As will be seen at B, this loose piece is slightly larger than the cut-out area of the pocket, but small enough to slip into the pocket.
- If the piece B is slipped into the pocket, the whole arrangement (the card and the loose piece) has the appearance of an ordinary card, when examined not too closely.

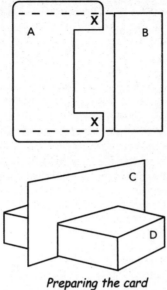

Preparing the card

1. You are now ready to start the trick. Tell your audience that you propose to cut a matchbox in half using a playing card. You pick up the card in question, put it across a matchbox and press down.
2. The loose piece B slides up into the pocket and your card rests on and around the matchbox (as shown at C), giving the appearance that you have cut the box (at D) into two.
3. On lifting the card from the box, the loose piece B is brought back into position by the strain being released from the elastic loops, and your cutting card appears to be quite innocent.

As long as you are not too close to your audience, this is a very impressive illusion.

THE MYSTERIOUS BOX

Special boxes can be bought from magic-supplies shops, but the one used for this trick is quite easy to make. You also need a pack of 'all-alike' cards.

- The box must be significantly larger than a playing card and have a hinged lid. The lid must be exactly the same as the lower part and the opening should halve the box.
- Two catches need to be fitted to the front edge of the box; one should lap over from the upper to the lower section and the other from the lower to the upper. This way, the box appears to be the right way up, whether it is stood on one face or the other.

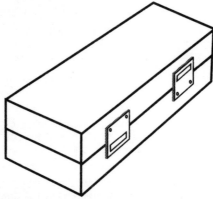

The box looks the right way up whichever face it stands on

- Next, you need a sheet of metal of exactly the same dimensions as the base of the box.
- Use matt black paint to paint the box inside and out and the two faces of the sheet.
- Make a copy of a card from the 'all-alike' pack, but enlarge it so that it is the same size as the metal sheet, on which it should now be stuck.

1. The trick is worked as follows. Make a fan with the 'all-alike' pack and offer it to a member of the audience. Ask him to choose a card. Make sure everyone sees what the card is, including you.
2. Open the box in full view of everybody and place the card inside. With much drama the catches are closed and a magic wand is passed over the box. Then the box is opened and the card has disappeared. In its place is a much larger picture of the original card, filling the bottom of the box completely.

Of course, the secret is understood from the preparations. Put the real card in the box one way and open it the other. The metal sheet conveniently drops to the bottom, whichever way the box is opened.

THE DISAPPEARING CARD

To make a card apparently disappear you will need a fake card made from a piece of acetate sheet, the sort used with an overhead projector. Hide this up your sleeve. You will also need a glass jug of yellowish liquid that you can pass off as lemonade.

1. Ask someone to select a card from a pack. Now, draw attention to your jug of 'lemonade'. Spin some tale about always having this with you as you are a strict teetotaller.

2. Produce a silk handkerchief and throw it over the card, which is held up in your left hand. Quick as lightning and assisted by your right hand, flick the card up your left sleeve and bring down the acetate in its place.

3. 'Now,' you say to somebody who seems amenable, 'can you feel the card?' Hold out the supposed card, shrouded by the handkerchief. Of course, he will say 'Yes'.

4. Place the handkerchief over the jug and allow it to fall in folds around it. Let go of the card and your audience sees the shape disappear. Wait a couple of seconds and then whip away the handkerchief, but show that it is empty.

The acetate card is nowhere to be seen

5. There is no card anywhere – not in the silken folds or in the jug. Where has it gone? The acetate being transparent and the liquid slightly yellow, there is nothing to see.

Don't let the idea of palming a card deter you from trying this trick. All it takes is practice.

MAGIC WRITING

There are many uses in magic for a 'thumb-writer' and it comes in many forms. The simplest one is a tiny piece of pencil lead pushed under your thumbnail. Alternatively, they can be bought from a magic shop in various guises, including flesh-coloured bands that fit over the ball of the thumb and entire false thumb tips with integral lead. The following trick makes use of a thumb-writer.

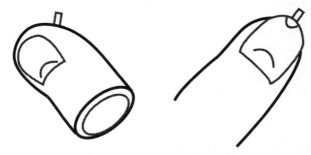

Examples of 'thumb-writers'

1. Invite a member of the audience to shuffle a pack of cards and then return it to you. Ask him for his initials.
2. Now borrow a pencil from another spectator and use it to mark any card with those initials, then give back the pencil. Of course, the writing here is pure pretence.
3. Now shuffle the cards again. Ask your spectator to name a card. Look through the pack, locate the card. This is when you take your chance to mark the initials on the card using the thumb-writer.
4. Now you hand over the card. The spectator will be amazed to see that his initials are written on it.

The borrowing and return of the pencil to an audience member only serves to increase dramatic effect. It's as well to have your own pencil handy, just in case.

Index